Magnets

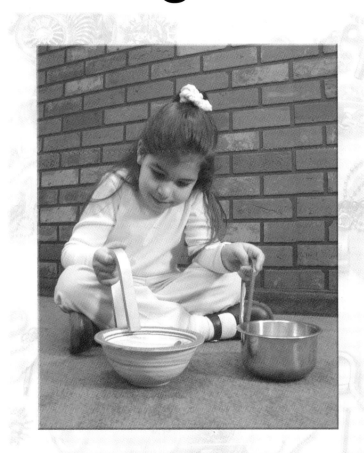

Story by Josie Stewart and Lynn Salem

Illustrations by Ryan Durney

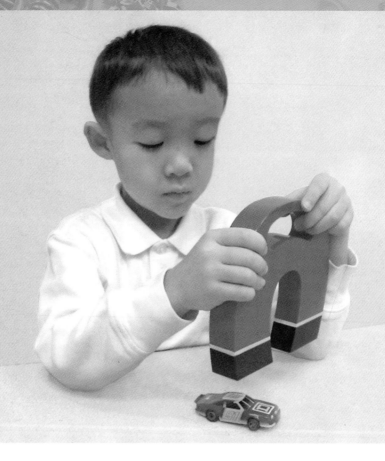

A car?
Yes.   No.

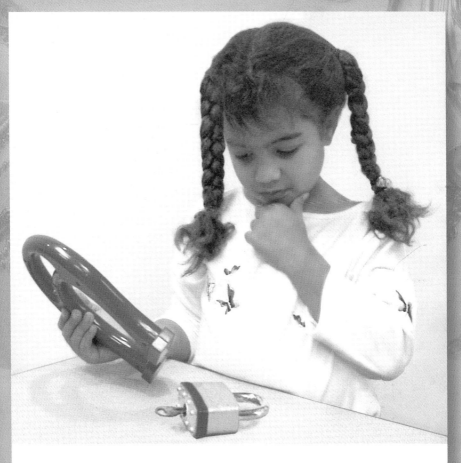

A lock?
Yes.　　　No.

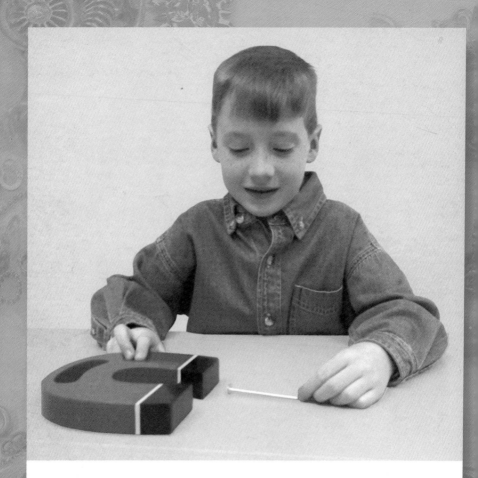

A nail?
Yes.   No.

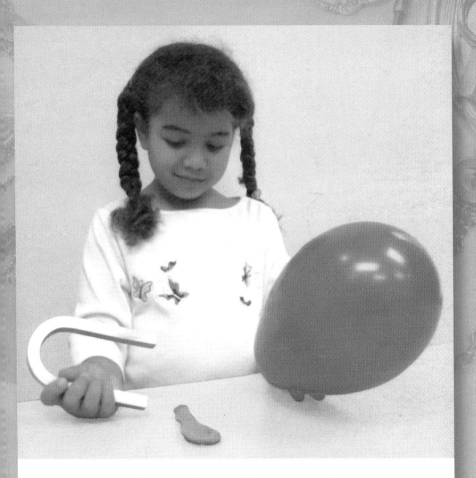

A balloon?
Yes.   No.

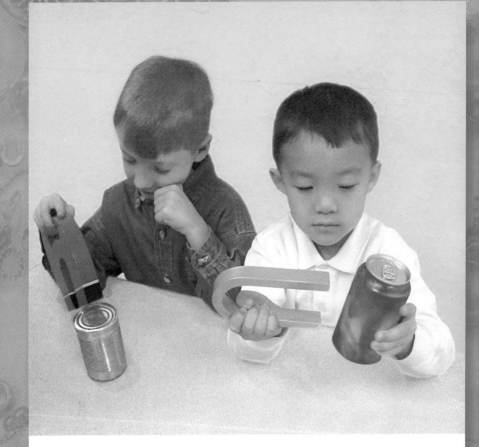

A can?
Yes.   No.

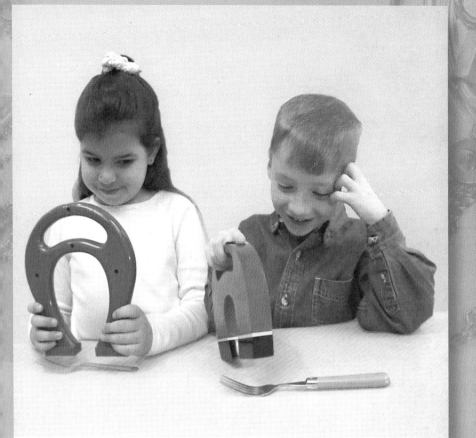

A fork?
Yes.   No.

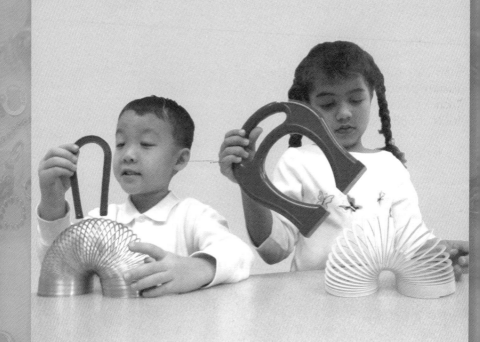

A toy?
Yes. **No.**